GUIDE TO LIFE

TO BUILD A HAPPY AND MEANINGFUL LIFE

NEELMANI BANSAL

Contents

Preface

This Book 'Guide to life illustrates about a story of a person named Abhyaas who was keenly passionate about a life.

One day, he was walking down the streets and thought that everyone is running after life, but only some of are living a truly life. So, he began his journey to search for a life that will bring peace, purpose and prosperity in his life.

This story is about a boy ,which aims us to achieve peace, happiness, calmness and prosperity.

This story will bring that how to live life better and make our way of living better.

I hope this book will bring happiness and calmness into your life by reading it.

LIVE YOUR LIFE TO YOUR FULLEST WITH
YOUR PASSION.

LIVE A BEAUTIFUL LIFE BY INVESTING IN
YOURSELF.

PEACE

CHAPTER ONE

There was a Boy named ABHYAAS, who was walking down the streets ,feeling anxious about the little things and was finding peace.

He was enjoying his own company, then suddenly he saw a group of people, who were together but not looking peace with themselves. They were talking , having a snack, but their faces seem, they can't find peace in that small chat.

Suddenly he saw a man, who was quietly sitting, beside the beach and was looking happy and that person seem that he has find a solitude in himself.

So the boy Abhyaas thought, that peace can't be found anywhere but within ourselves.

The boy named Abhyaas went to that person and sat next beside to him and asked, 'You look so happy, so peaceful, what is the secret behind that.

The man replied '' Ahh Boy, Peace is within ourselves, it is not found in external things or materialistic things.

When, we are satisfy with ourselves that what we are doing is right, it doesn't matter what society thinks, you do your job, without thinking that what everyone else will think, when you wake up, start your day with a smile, do all the things that makes you happy, that makes you feel alive, and when you go to bed, there is satisfaction inside you that you did your best, Next day you will be better from this day.

When you think of this, when you do this, irrespective of what society thinks, you will attain peace, because you have reached that amount of satisfaction that bring peace to your life.

After listening to this, Boy went home and he sat amidst the nature in his balcony, took a deep breath started to realize his own potential. He started taking gratitude in little things, for his breath, for his family, roof over his head, clean water, food on the table.

By practicing gratitude each day, he was feeling good day by day.

He started to make Journal and wrote down those things which make him alive, the things which make him happy.

Then Next day, he woke up and plan his day according to him.

He eat healthy breakfast, meditate then start doing those things which make him happy.

Abhyaas liked music very much. He was keenly interested in playing Guitar.

He started to play Guitar for several hours. By Practicing Guitar, because of his passion of playing Guitar, he just drove in the melody of tuning of Guitar sound. He began to enjoy that process.

By each day, he woke up excited, because he found a true passion for his life – Music.

By identifying our true passion, we enjoy our routine more and start enjoying our each day of our life.

Make your each day countable.

Find one thing in your life which bring immerse joy into your life, By Practicing that one thing, and gratitude for little things into your life, your life become yours.

When you block the noises of your surroundings, you find your true passion and purpose into your life, which will bring immerse peace and satisfaction.

Now, when Abhyaas played music everyday, not only he experienced joy, his surroundings also become joyful. When anyone of the people sat next to him, they also feel joyful. This is the power of positivity and joyfulness inside our life, which impact other people's lives also.

So if we are happy and positive within ourselves, our surroundings also become joyful.

People seem happy and peaceful when they sit next to us.

Abhyaas sister used to remain stressed about her studies. One evening Abhyaas was playing guitar. His soft melody attracted his sister and she sat next beside to him. After listening to his music, she forget about her worries and she also become peaceful and joyful.

That's the power of positivity.

After playing Guitar, Abhyaas started to participate in various things in his College, which was related to music.

His love for passion, become his daily work.

He participated in various stage performances and soon his work get better day by day.

His work was praised by many of his classmates and his friends. Soon slowly, his self confidence began to build up.

He started to search for opportunities that will make him a better person day by day.

So, by finding our true passion and by increasing the performance in that passion, gradually make us a confident person.

You can find your true passion or you can start anything which bring joy and satisfaction to your life, and practice that task everyday to enhance your performance.

Then see, a new magic coming into your life.

To maintain peace

So, when things go wrong, People start to lose temper, because they cannot control themselves. And when they lose temper, distortion occurs in our lives.

So, to maintain peace in any situation, you have to maintain a habit to control yourself.

Abhyaas learn this technique from his mother. Whenever she gets anger, she don't get violent, instead she do her hobby that makes her happy and her hobby was cooking food.

So Abhyaas learn this technique from her.

Whenever he gets angry in any thing, he start playing guitar, which suddenly calms his mind, and he again come to peace.

For this, you have to develop a habit.

This technique don't work in single time.

You have to repeat this process again and again till this habit become a part of your life.

Now, not only he played Guitar, but he wanted to learn so many things.

He wanted to explore that, what he can do his best in a thing.

So he tried many things like painting, playing a sport, or playing some other instrument of music.

Suddenly while experimenting with this, he start to get interest in playing tennis.

He began to like that sport.

Beside playing Guitar, he also began to play tennis.

He began to enjoy this process.

So, after few months of practice of tennis, he made a firm grip on it and it made him a commander of the tennis.

So, he developed these beautiful habits like to be grateful everyday, to make healthy habits, to sharp his brain everyday so that whenever he go to bed at night he go with a smile and satisfaction.

This become his journey of life.

Learning is a very healthy process. It enhances our capacity and sharpen our mind.

At any stage you are start developing a healthy habit of learning.

Learn each and everything from life, whether from experiences or things.

Learn good habits from each other.

When we try to learn something, it increases the capacity and thinking of our mind.

Don't learn because you just have a certain goal. Learn because it is a enjoyable process.

Learn till the end of your life, till you breathe, and then see wonderful things coming into your life.

These are the little tiny habits, that make our life wonderful.

Apply this tiny little habits daily into your life and see how life transformation begins.

Enjoy the little moments of the life because these are the most precious ones.

When you sit and talk with your grandparents, listen to their stories, listen to their experiences and their life lessons.

It will also teach you something.

Do a chit chat with your parents for a few minutes at least. Try to understand them.

See their perspective of life from their point of view. These little things will increase and strength the bondage of Love.

Try this out.

So from above there are plenty of wonderful things which makes our life happier and better.

Try to do small tiny habits into your life, which will bring huge peace and success into your life.

Day to Day, Abhyaas performance was increasing. He was not doing well in his life but he was also feeling peace and satisfaction within himself.

As days become passed, his mind now wanted new things to learn everyday. He has developed a habit of this to learn something new everyday.

His mind become sharper day by day.

One day, Abhyaas was sitting on his terrace, and he saw a plane flying above him.

He felt curious about plane that how did that plane fly in the sky against of gravity. How did the pilot manage the traffic above clouds.

Whatever the question arise, ask again and again whether it is silly or not.

Asking questions increase our curiosity.

There was a vision which he had seen in his eyes to fly high, not sitting in an Airplane but by riding it.

When we see any dream or wish to acquire it, then trust me you can manifest anything, you want in your life.

Just take a glance at your dream and say it, that I can do it.

Then start working on it.

And your goal can be achieved by your daily habits.

Make your each day memorable.

Start with daily Habits.

Be discipline and consistent on each day.

Whenever you wake up in the morning, look into the mirror and say, You are the Best, You can do it.

Treat yourself lovable.

Invest in yourself.

Your biggest investment is in you.

You can give everything you want.

You can shape the life, according to your plan, that how you spend your 24hrs day.

Next Habit, you can develop a habit of enthusiasm.

When you wake up in the morning, be excited about the day.

When you work with enthusiasm an impulse of electricity generates in your Body and you can work more efficiently.

Make this a habit of your daily routine.

If in your routine if you play any sport, begin with enthusiasm.

It will transfer the energy towards your work.

Now let me start about hurdles which can come while you do any type of work whether achieving Goal or doing some kind of activity.

Don't get panic while hurdles come.

Breathe calmly and think quietly that how this problem can be solved.

Learn the mistakes from it and try to never repeat those mistakes in your work.

Start seeing failures as an opportunity

And learn from those failures.

Don't try to judge yourself that you can't do this or you are not capable of it.

Rather think how can I improve from this.

So start seeing failures as your stepping stone for your success.

Your Goal depend upon that how you see this opportunity as a hurdle.

Whether grow from it or think for it.

Choice is yours.

Now when things seem wrong, have some patience and try to remain cool in that situation.

Give some time to yourself and to that situation. After some time you will find a solution to that problem. Patience is the greatest key that everyone should practice.

Everything comes with practice whether it is patience or something else.

The boy named Abhyaas use to do this technique of developing patience.

Whenever the situation is not according to him, he left the situation for a while and take some time to think.

He arrives the solution after taking some time.

I think each and everything needs time to build something whether it is relationship or your Goal.

The boy was going in the right direction. He was investing in himself.

He was making his better version of himself day by day.

He was exploring himself and finding that where are his weakest points lies.

He began to search for that.

Its easy to find errors in others but it is difficult to find errors in ourselves that where we are going wrong.

By improving yourself in your daily tasks or by becoming better human being, you can give everything to yourself and to this society.

Sometimes our Peace gets disturbed by external circumstances. People tend to shift their Goal on the basis of their external circumstances.

In order to get not disturb one should be firmly dedicated to their Goal or to their task. If they are dedicated and committed towards their Goal then nothing can stop from achieving their success.

You have to firmly cool your mind and adapt to your surroundings.

Because as you know Charles Darwin once said that Survival of the fittest.

Organisms that are better adapted to their environment are best suited to survive. The Boy sat quietly beside his window and he was feeling satisfaction and peace within himself. Thus he knew that he is going right direction.

When we feel satisfied within ourselves and with our work that we do that understand this that you are going in the right direction.

Beside all this try to develop as many skills as you can.

Skill related to money.

Skill related to hobby that make you feel smile and relax.

It is important to develop skills especially in youth to be productive everyday.

Many times we are surrounded by so many people, there are various mixtures of people Positive and negative.

These both type of People influence our lives. So its very important to surrounded by those people whose energy is contagious and positive, those will uplift you and help you in achieving your Dreams.

So choose wisely.

There was a competition in Abhyaas School, a group competition.

He have to select a group of individuals to work on a particular Task.

So he thought that team work is very important. So he have to choose his team very carefully.

He selected those people who were positive and enthusiastic towards their work.

He selected for their team that can collaborate into a wonderful team.

So by selected that team each day was a learning day because there was something to learn from each individual from the team which can maximize their winning performance.

They show cooperation and dedicated their energy to work.

So, its all about the perseverance, dedication, sincerity that makes a certain Goal or task done.

Networking is a crucial step in building a achievable Goal.

Start making connections, build Positive relationships and stay connected to those who make you feel worthy and valued.

Surround yourself with People who value you who is empathetic and kind towards you.

So by proper networking and dedicated towards his Goal, the boy started feeling Happy.

Your destiny is not written but you create your destiny by creating healthy habits and Positive relationships.

Make it a Habit to develop all these things in your regular routine.

Stick to these things which shift us towards our Goal.

If you want to create your destiny then you have to plan it accordingly.

Make your Dreams come true. Another quality of life you can have is to spend some time with your Parents.

Talk to them, Listen to their stories and their life experiences, try to build a positive relationship with them.

Having a positive relationship with your parents not only enhance your quality of life but also it build the trust between you and your parents.

Make them understand your life and understand their life also.

Understand their perspective of life and then by spending time with them you see immense growth in terms of experiences.

Self Love is also another key to obtain Peace and Happiness.

Always see yourself that you are worthy and capable. If you wish something then you can make that wish come true.

You have all the abilities which are required to succeed.

You just only have to practice self Love.

Whenever you wake up in the morning look into the mirror and say to yourself with a smile that you are worthy and unique and you can achieve your dreams by regular practice and with consistency.

Discipline and consistency will help you to achieve anything.

So the boy was in his school yet and he was exploring himself and seeking opportunities to grow more and be a better version of himself.

He practice daily and he has grown into a better version of himself that led to discovery of his ambition that he want to become a Pilot and want to ride an airplane.

So don't follow the crowd that this exam has many competitors so I want to pursue that rather than explore yourself that in which thing you can give your best and follow that thing.

Follow your passion.

The boy was so excited about his dream but he was more excited to work for that.

He knew that time is very precious so he wisely utilize his time very efficiently.

His habits make him a powerful person.

He started researching about his dream that how to get there.

His vision was totally on his dream so he started making a map to get in that destination.

So by making a map to your destination and arranging the tools which are required to get there makes a journey easier and easy to achieve because you know that what to do when and how.

Finally the boy was graduating from his school and as you know he has become a better version of himself.

He was ready to chase his dream to become a Pilot.

As we don't get what we want but we get that who we are.

To achieve something you have to be like that person, that level of thinking, that level of attitude, that level of skills.

When you become like your dream person whether in habits, whether in way of living, destiny come together to fulfill your dream.

So focus on becoming that person and you will see that how magically you will get your dream job.

Next is when you become that type of person then many fears will come along your side, it could be of any of your fears

Fears related to your trauma, related to any incident but overcome that fear.

When you overcome that fear then nothing can stop you from achieving your destination.

Just keep focusing and enjoy the process.

You will surely achieve success.

There are part of lives which we are connected either through human being or to some thing by which our emotions are connected. When that person is hurt or something happened to that thing, there is suddenly change in our emotions.

Its ok to feel emotions, to express emotions.

Emotions make us a beautiful human being. It channelize our brain that the thing which we are connected is so important to our life.

Don't let that thing or person move away from your life.

Make a special place in your heart for them.

During our darkest and good times these relationships will play a huge role in our lives. So stay connected to them while you chase your dreams.

Celebrate your wins with them and share your things when it get dark. It will empower you.

Live your life to the fullest and enjoy the moments of this beautiful life which will teach you so many things.

Explore yourself and enjoy the moments while chasing your dreams.

Now the boy was ready for his preparation for his exam for airlines.

But before preparation for his exam he did so many research regarding his ambition his goals.

He had made his personality for his exam.

He knew if he want to crack the exam then he should think like that.

He has created his strong mindset for all the hurdles that he will face during his ambition.

This exam was not a preparation of one year rather than a preparation of habits he developed in his entire journey from beginning to till yet.

So he created a timetable for his routine that he will stick to this time table with discipline and consistency.

When he will follow that routine consistently then only he can succeed.

If you want to crack any exam then be consistent about your journey.

Time is very precious. Don't waste your time in unnecessary things and stay active by doing healthy habits.

When the boy has developed a healthy habits he also transformed his brain to stronger limits. He know that he is capable of achieving higher dreams.

So whenever he thinks that he is getting stressed he know that what he have to do,

He picked up his hobby of playing guitar and soon he get fully recharged.

So his healthy habit not even recharge him but make a strong connections in his brain to focus better.

So start choosing that habits that empower your focus, so that you can focus with full determination.

Beside this he developed a habit of eating good food, good food means nutritious food that will keep his brain sharp and his body fit.

So he practiced day and night for his preparation beside keeping his focus on his health. Suddenly he realized that if he want to achieve a highest rank then he should enjoy his process of preparation.

He began to enjoy the process of his journey. Whenever he feel tired he would spend time with his loved ones because these connections should be preserved so that our journey becomes easy and highly efficiently.

If we want to achieve something then team work is very important.

So work as a team. That will empower you.

So the boy made his entire routine based on all these things, not only he was getting satisfied but he was enjoying his process and feeling grateful for what he was doing.

So the main aim of our life is inner satisfaction.

If we are satisfied with ourselves, our ambition then there is nothing to worry about because it gives a sense of pleasure in doing all these things as these things naturally flow, you don't have to force anything.

Just having a calm mindset can remove all the difficulties of your life.

Just be like water.

Calm.

For achieving any dream you just have to get focus, deep work have to be done in order to get success.

For better focus you just have to set habits of developing good focus like meditation, nature walk, not doing multitasking and only focusing on a single task at a time.

Try this for a months and see magic in your results.

Always keep believing that you can do everything, you are not the water in the ocean but you are the ocean.

Just invest in yourself.

The biggest investment is you.

Keep growing and enjoy the little things in your life that God has given to you.

So as you keep evolving, certain failures will also come but you have to embrace your failures and start seeing them as a step of success.

Don't fear from failure but rather embrace it and learn from the mistakes.

HAPPINESS

So when you have reached your limit potential then suddenly happiness follows you.

Happiness is a Habit, cultivate it.

You don't have to follow happiness but you have to create it each day and make it a habit.

People think that by achieving certain goal or by buying certain things, only you can find happiness but after you reached your destination you will feel that happiness is an illusion, rather it should be created on your daily basis and you can see changes in your life that you have become a happy person.

I think happiness is in the process of your journey, it do not lies on your final destination but it really lies on your path in which you are walking.

So instead chasing happiness in your final destination, embrace it in your journey and your process of achieving your dream becomes easy and you will also not get to know that you have reached your destination with flying colors.

If you enjoy your learnings and always get excited about your work that today will be a big day, then your dreams will chase you not you will chase your dreams. The boy was chasing his day to get better each day and his happiness was chasing him because he was enjoying the process.

He was not worried about his result rather than he was making his each day countable by pushing himself beyond his limits.

Yes, he was getting better day by day and this thing made him more happy then anything else.

He was learning from his mistakes and giving his hundred percent to his dream.

For achieving any dream you have to be like water, calm, when there is calmness, there is confidence, you have to listen to your heart and believe in yourself that you can do it.

Finally the boy 6 months have passed in his preparation and he was feeling confidence not about the results but rather about his preparation that he is giving hundred percent to his dream.

Each day he woke up with excitement that today will be a new day and he will do anything to make his day better day then before.

Beside his preparation, he was grateful to the little things in his life which make him happy day by day.

He didn't chase happiness rather he choose happiness and cultivate it by looking and to be grateful each day for his family, for sunlight, for his food on the table.

Be grateful for what you have because what you have is precious.

So smile each day and bring positivity and sunshine into your life.

Time began to passed and the boy was nearer to his exam, sometimes we feel certain obstacles into our way and this leads to anxiety, overthinking.

For that you just have to trust the process and go with the flow rather than overthinking.

To compete this process certain steps can be take like meditation, yoga or some relaxing techniques like reading a book or playing with your pet.

These things can certainly calm you and bring you in your original state.

Thus have faith in process and overcome your hurdles by simply calming yourself.

Remember that calmness is a strong quality, those who can practice calmness can do anything in their life.

So just relax and trust the process.

The boy suddenly passed his entire year in his preparation, then next month he was about to give his exam which was very near. He was feeling anxious but rather to be anxious he was practicing himself to calm down.

Slowly and slowly he developed a habit to to be calm in every situation.

When you start to calm down and when you become like water calm and peaceful, certain things also become clear to you.

He has practiced his calmness and before every test he use to give he develop to be calm before giving any test.

When his mind come in calm stage, he was more focused, more able to see things clearly.

When certain things can't seem to understand then give a pause and take rest.

Remember when you get tired , take rest not quit.

Take plenty of sleep when you are unable to decide something.

Sleeping improves brain connections and improve your well being.

Take minimum amount of sleep at least for 8 hours.

Do not compensate your sleep for anything.

Sleep is important medicine for mind, as it improve level of thinking and will make you more focus on your task.

So this is the way to combat stress and anxiety.

Days have passed and the boy was near to his exam, he was almost prepared and ready to give his exam.

The Boy appeared for exam after one year of preparation and before giving his exam most important thing he done was to calm his mind and attain peace from within.

So he meditate for a while and then appeared for his exam.

He try his best in attempting the questions which was asked in a paper.

He give all the answers confidentially and with full focus.

He gave his exam and he came home and relaxed for a while, and began to think patience is the key.

Now he just only have to wait for the results and wait for the next opportunity.

We should never miss opportunities, whenever any opportunity come or knock to our door we should always say yes, you can postpone that opportunity but never miss it, because opportunities makes our personality.

Although the boy was feeling relaxed after giving his exam but his wish to learn throughout life didn't stop him.

After one year of his preparation he again wanted to start something that he can learn from.

So he started playing some sport whether tennis or basketball.

Always challenge your brain to learn something everyday.

It mentally strong the mind and it will make new connections of neurons that will make your brain healthy which is important for achieving high level of success.

Days have passed and the boy was eagerly waiting for his results.

He was hoping for best and his family was also waiting because they saw that how hard work their son has done overall his life to attain success.

When we hope there are new possibilities of life which make us dream even higher and that make us move throughout our life.

So always have positive hopes that whatever be the result I will try to learn from that result rather then judging the result.

So after so much eagerly of hard work and dedication, he didn't stop practicing his hobbies which have make him a better person in terms of growth.

He usually played his guitar, watch educational videos, play his tennis.

If you want to achieve anything then behave and develop a habits like a King or Queen.

Build their attitude in terms of how they react in failure times, their strategy of winning and their daily habits that is recognized as a King.

Don't settle for less, always dream bigger.

When we feel inner satisfaction that we did our best and try to do best and to learn things in any stage, then nothing can beat us.

It gives immense happiness and joy when we learn new things.

Try to learn new things everyday.

You can learn anything by sitting at home also from your mother, from your sister, from your granny.

That how they live their life and sort out their problems whether it is small or big.

Try to learn from your elders, it will nourish you.

Now days were passing and the boy was enjoying his days with his family, with his friends and with his hobbies.

He began to appreciate and thankful to the little things in his life that whatever he has, he is grateful to all these things.

He began to enjoy little things in his life and was fully prepared for his result.

He began to thought that whatever will be the result he would surely learn some thing from that result whether good or bad.

He will never lose hope and would never give up despite all the difficulties.

Now the result was about to come, so it will be a huge day for the boy that his result was coming.

He crossed his fingers, took a deep breaths and hoping to be positive and always he thought that whatever will be the result he would learn something from it.

So the day arrives and his family and he was waiting for the result, finally the time came, his mother was praying to God, his father was walking here and there because on this day his son would get a new life.

A biggest opportunity for the family, for the boy also because if he cleared the exam, he would enter into new phase of his life, biggest responsibilities would enter into his life, and he would even dream higher, because we should never stop dreaming.

When we attain a certain height then we should dream that how far I can go from this place to the biggest place, far better from this place.

When we develop such type of thinking, then success would always follow us till we breath.

Success is not about a certain goal but it should be a life long learning process. Finally the day has arrived and he checked his result.

When he put his eyes on the screen, he was not shocked, not frustrated but he took a deep breath and sigh a relief.

Yes the result was not good rather then the result was negative.

But the boy was not frustrated, he just sat in a corner and began to thought that what was his mistakes in the preparation process.

He didn't get frustrated that how could he not pass this exam after so much his hard work that he had done in his entire year, but rather he was in his full hope that he would never give up and will learn from his mistakes that where he went bad, he didn't blame the situation nor he blame himself that he couldn't crack this exam but rather he began to think that how the things could go better and how he can learn from this result.

This is the mindset that successful people build.

He took a pause and then took a break to refresh himself from all these things for a while and took a deep breath that what went wrong and how can he correct it.

To calm his mind he went for a short trip with his friends and when he came back from there he organized a plan that what was his mistakes in his preparation.

He collected all those mistakes and planned according to it.

He recognized that this strategy will not work and rather then giving up he should follow another strategy to crack this exam.

He sat and worked on those mistakes that he did in his exam and organized a plan map that to reach his destination he should follow another path to reach his destination.

So rather then giving up we should work on our mistakes and shift our strategy to work on that particular object or target.

If we want to succeed then fear of failure should be remove from our life.

Because this fear of failure will never let us succeed.

If you fall get up and rise, it doesn't matter how many times you fall of, matter is how many times you get up.

That hunger of achieving something will always head you towards your destination despite that how difficult is that destination.

So keep fighting with your dreams until you achieve them.

He attained calmness again, because calmness is necessary in order to decrease the entropy (entropy is state of disordered). So after cooling and coming into calmer state, he again participated in race, the race was with himself that how far he is better from yesterday.

Don't compare your journey with someone else, regard compete with yourself, improve your weakness and stabilize your strength which is essential for high performance.

Always strive the hunger of success, because that hunger will eventually lead you to success.

The level of patience that the boy was showing is commendable.

He was patience that one day he will reach there where he wanted to reach.

Pain of discipline is better then pain of regret.

He was trying his best again to give his outstanding performance and he was astonished to see himself and felt happy that he has not lost his enthusiasm.

Don't give up without losing the enthusiasm because that will give you enormous amount of energy in your field of work progress.

This is the way to get up after you get failed, when life knocks us down then get up and show yourself into the mirror that whatever life brings challenges into my life, I will fight for myself, for my dreams and will get there at any cost by learning through the process.

This simple mindset will eventually will be your success point in your life.

So worry less and action more towards your Goal because one day you will make it and you will be proud that you didn't give up and follow your dreams.

The boy sat in the solitude and began his preparation again. This time he was working on his mistakes that he did in his preparation or in exam that where he went wrong and how he could correct those mistakes.

Eventually he didn't lose his temper and gather all his courage that is needed in the preparation mode because that purpose of flying in the air kept him going.

To kept going that hidden purpose that you are getting prepare for the exam should be kept encouraging because only that purpose will give you strength to keep you going.

Ask yourself every time question that why did you started and why do you want to go in that particular destination.

When that thought you will keep encouraging then nobody can stop you from reaching your destination.

Several days have passed and the boy was again preparing for his dream with more enthusiasm.

This enthusiasm when his family sees, they get very proud, they didn't get proud that their boy will be selected but they were proud that despite the failure the boy show courage to face his failure and stand up for his dreams.

So if you want to make your parents proud then show enthusiasm each day, whether it is work or something else.

When you show enthusiasm, the happiness will reflect on their faces and they will be very proud that you didn't give up.

This journey become his habit and he was proud of himself that he didn't give up.

Everyday he hard work triple to ensure that his previous mistakes should not be repeated and this time to make sure to give his 100 percent.

Sometimes many doubts came in his mind that is this will be fruitful or not then he realized why he started this journey and he always keep moving despite the obstacles.

To be grateful and showing gratitude is very important in any journey.

I think these are not the hardest times but a part of the journey that comes in everyone's life.

So difference is that how a person deals with failure, that is the true test.

If you are not afraid of failure then you can climb higher.

Don't let fear come along your way in your step of success.

Climb the mountains if you want to go at highest peak and overcome all your fears.

Sometimes in life what we want do not get easily because easy things don't give us strength.

Difficult things gives us strength and it makes us a human being that can wish to dream even higher.

When we get strength in the most challenging times there is what character develops and our true potential is seen in those times. Many days has been passed and the boy was smiling and enjoying the whole process.

It was difficult to start again but our true potential lies in how we face our failures.

Fail many times but get up stronger.

Almost when boy began to realized that he have learned so many things in life and one lesson he has learnt from failure that in any situation not giving up is the best mindset for successful people.

So learn from the failures and start again.

Because starting again is what makes you champion.

So go after your dreams without any fear.

When you face your fears, your all fears will get away from your life.

Just see yourself that you are bigger then your failures.

Many times when things get difficult then don't see that how the things are difficult but rather see that you are bigger than this.

When you realize your worthiness that you are capable of doing things despite of these difficulties then the problems will seem small to you.

Take step by step and trust yourself that if you can dream it, then you can achieve it.

Few months have passed and the boy was becoming stronger mentally because when you get up after you fall then you become stronger and stronger day by day.

You become wise because you learn from the difficulties and face them.

When you face your challenges you become bold person which is very important for making your dream to come into reality.

So whenever difficulties come, don't run away from them rather than face them and become a more wise person not only in life but also in various performances which you want to participate. This is exactly what life is, we don't get what we want, sometimes life want to grind us so that we can shine.

When we face our difficulties then our character develops and who overcome the obstacles is what a true character shows.

So indeed of thinking that what life you get, start building your life because your life is yours.

How we shape our lives depend on our daily habits, how we talk, what we think, what kind of mindset our is.

Try to control these things and your life will be according to you.

These magic pills will surely keep you ahead in life.

In life it doesn't matter that how fast you walk, rather it matters that how wisely you take small steps.

That determine your determination.

For that you have to be in discipline mode.

When you are in discipline, everything comes to you flow naturally.

So bring discipline into your life and see how this discipline will take you ahead.

Don't seek motivation but rather see discipline in your daily life.

As our life throw challenges, we grow from them and eventually it make our life more meaningful.

So challenges make our life even more exciting and is essential for our growth process.

So don't fear from your challenges rather than embrace your challenges.

When you love your challenges and ready to play with them, then it becomes easier for you to cross your hurdles and it will make you smarter day by day.

Step out of your comfort zone and grow through what you get in life and make a best of it.

It doesn't matter what ingredients you get in life to shape your life.

Matter is how you use that ingredients in a best way to optimize your life.

Choice is yours.

When we feel stuck in our lives that what to do and what to not, then listen to your heart because that heart will keep you get motivated for your higher purpose in your life.

So worry less and do more because at the end of your journey you will proudly say that you didn't give up.

Always keep hoping for the best.

This time the boy learned the process of learning and he make sure to not repeat his mistakes.

So he was organizing his day plan according to him and he worked on those field in which he was scoring less or he was in weaker area.

He worked in his weaker areas to make that strong and working more on his stronger fields to make them even more better to score more.

So by giving more time to your stronger area to enhance your performance and work on your weaker areas to get in a safe zone.

This strategy is really helpful.

Because in the strong area you are capable of achieving more.

So work on that more so that you can beat any exam by excellency in your particular field.

The boy was consistent in his daily routine.

He acted discipline in his daily schedule.

When we are in discipline mode, everything seems to flow naturally.

Discipline leads to high level of motivation.

So don't seek motivation, seek discipline in your daily routine.

Life will give you many obstacles but you have to cross your obstacles in a very calm manner.

With calmness, just be like water calm and free from all your worries.

When you become like a water then eventually you will find a way to cross all your hurdles.

Life is very simple.

Just live your life and love the process.

Don't give up.

Because losers are not those who have nothing, but losers are those who give up.

So to keep winning never give up.

So this was it, the entire process of the boy journey from learning to experience things in life, he grew up from all these things.

When we are determined that what we want to do and what we want from life things becomes clear and that seem to serve us a purpose.

So purpose in life is very essential for a meaningful life.

When you have a purpose then you can go in the right direction, regardless of how long is that direction.

So find your purpose and go for it.

Because you are born to do miracle things.

Just trust yourself and have faith that one day you will going to say that you made it.

One day you will be proud that you didn't give up.

Always hope for the best and keep working towards it.

The Time is crucial factor for anyone's growth.

When we value time we value ourselves.

So optimize your time according to your priorities.

When you value your time, you can take control of your present.

So start having boundaries with yourself too.

Make a list that in how many instances and on which things your time is consuming.

Consider them are these activities are a important part of my life.

Are they are playing a crucial role in the part of my growth.

When you start considering these things that who you spend your most time with, which type of habits you build in your life.

Many things become clear and you start valuing yourself.

Know the importance of this precious time.

Time is precious but live your life also.

Do things that you love most.

Participate in various activities that bring you joy, that help you in growth.

Put yourself in uncomfortable situations.

Don't remain in comfort zone.

Comfort zone always prevent you from growth.

Seek chances that will build you with yourself.

Discover yourself.

Embrace yourself.

Explore yourself.

The unique quality is always present in you.

Identify that what is unique in you and gather all your sources to use your uniqueness and find inspiration from it.

Each individual is unique and has some qualities that he can serve themselves and to this world.

Don't copy the world rather than create your own magic to fill your rainbow.

One day you will shine like a Rainbow.

Now the story begins with the boy who was pursuing his dreams.

Meanwhile when he was doing his best, he almost encounter his fears.

When you encounter your fears then you reach into that field where you can see clearly your dreams.

When you face your fears, you feel to begin a sense of calm and suddenly you begin to realize that fear is only in your mind.

Fear is no real but it is just a imagination of your mind that plays a trick on you that fear is real and you can't do it.

But when you face them whether it is your weakness or your limits to reach to sky, try to face them.

One time your body will shake but facing your fears again and again will destroy all your fears and you will say to yourself that what I was afrading about is so simple.

It was just a fear that was controlling me and my limits.

You are beyond your fears.

So break the wall and reach to the limit of the sky.

After facing them and winning over your fears you will feel that what I wanted from my journey becomes simple, because those fears were stopping you to reach towards your Goal.

Don't complain because when you complain, you make yourself into a victim, when you speak out you are in your Power.

So decide whether you want power or you want to make yourself into a victim.

The boy was doing all his best to reach his destination.

He was more focused on his journey that how to make his journey more beautiful and more inspiring just not to him but to all those who was watching his success story.

One night the boy was suddenly get up from sleep and ran to his mother.

When he saw his mother is sleeping, he quietly went there and observe that how peacefully her mother was sleeping.

Similarly he realize that her mother don't expect anything from her family.

She gives unconditionally love and care to her family.

Similarly we should not expect the results.

Because something which we love should be done without any expectations.

And when we do anything without expectation the result is automatically becomes positive.

This happens so because we get indulge in our work with so much focus and with so much passion that it automatically works.

Work should be done with a passion.

When we are passionate about something then unexpectically the result come positive.

So focus on the journey and when your journey seems beautiful with ups and downs then you are winning guys.

So make your journey beautiful and count the moments that you create in your journey.

There are certain moments in our life when we want to give up.

Certain situations make us to think like that but at the end of the day you will feel regret that why did you give up.

So handle the obstacles with calm and patience and the obstacles and the situations will be seem flawless in front of you.

Just have patience and think that why you have started this chapter.

Write your life beautiful.

This is your story.

Take a pen and write your own story.

Claim it.

When you starting developing patience then you will make a habit of developing patience.

Everything can be develop whether a good habit or a bad habit.

It only depends on you that which habit you want to develop.

Either develop a habit that will raise you or develop a habit that will lower you for meeting your goals.

Choice is yours.

Choose wisely.

Act smartly.

So the boy was on his second phase of his life and he was just enjoying the same phase again.

To do better you have to be better day by day in terms of every aspect.

Just do your work efficiently and boldly and always stand firm on your decisions that one day what you have thought to become will come true.

When you believe in yourself then the entire universe will believe in you.

Years have been passed and the boy was thinking that one day he will be so proud of himself that he didn't give up and despite all the obstacles he tried so hard to go for his target.

When we don't focus on the target rather than focus on the journey and try to make our garden beautiful then butterflies will automatically chase the garden.

It's the nature of the butterflies, they attract only in a beautiful garden.

So try to make your each day beautiful.

Step by step your each day will make you a beautiful years that will make your beautiful life.

Certain things are very simple in life.

When we didn't understand anything just don't try to understand the things.

Just keep calm and try to observe things.

When you observe things in a smart way complicated things also get simple.

So don't panic when you can't sort anything, just sit and relax.

It will get automatically resolve when you solved the problems in a simple and in cool manner.

Complicated things can only be solved by simple means.

And it will give you the beautiful answer. When life seems unpredictable that what to do in this stage, just remind yourself that this will not last forever.

Bad times will certainly go and the sun will shine again.

Just keep moving with full enthusiasm and challenge your fears everyday.

When you challenge your fears then fears will run away in front of you and there will be a new strong version of you will be there.

You will be so proud to yourself.

Just make sure to proud yourself everyday be it not giving up and try harder and harder till you succeed.

When you make yourself proud then you will also make your parents proud.

Just keep getting better day by day.

Year after year when you get better day by day you feel nice towards you, to your surroundings.

Just get better in terms of health, in terms of life, in terms of your goals.

When you start setting your tiny habits in your daily life then these tiny habits will lead towards your goal.

Just focus on your daily habits and eventually you will reach to your destination.

Besides healthy habits you have to take care of your Health.

Because health is wealth.

If you are fit then your body will do more work.

If your mind is active then you can focus better.

So train your body and mind to keep healthy.

Eat nutritious food and exercise a lot.

Participate in various sports activities whether it is swimming, playing tennis.

Just move your body.

Your health should be the priority.

So build your health and wealth.

The Boy finally appeared for his exam again with firm confidence and with positivity that he would give his hundred percent this time.

He meditate for a while and gave his exam.

He gave his exam in a relaxed and in a calm stage because whatever we do we should do each task in a calm manner and with positivity.

When we think like a water and become like a water, in a flow state then everything run according to us because chaos mind only create difficulties.

But calm mind create hopes and enthusiasm which make our work even more energetic and enjoyable.

This time the boy attempted his exam and now he returned home with a sense of relief that he again gave his hundred percent.

He learnt from his previous mistakes and ready to overcome his life with many form of challenges.

He relaxed and took a break from all of these.

He went for a trek that he always wanted to do.

Sometimes spending and relapsing time in nature make us free from worries and it bring us a positive energy around us.

Something is beautiful in the nature that make us feel alive on this earth.

It is so because nature gives us needy things to survive like food and water.

When we feel the nature then we can feel it because nature is real, free from artificial things.

Nature is pure so when we enter into nature or spend time in nature it make us forget about all the worries and give a sense of relief.

So outdoor activities positively recharge us and make us grounded and humble.

When we see leaves falling on earth then we realize that everything is temporary.

Nature always give something to learn that how to adapt with the surroundings, how to remain calm like a water.

How to stay grounded like a tree and yet it is growing and feeding human beings in the form of fruits, in the form of shelter.

So try to learn each and everything from nature.

We can learn so many things from our surroundings, yet to discover.

Everything's aligns with the nature.

Nature gives us sense of calm.

It makes us believe that joy can be found in little things too.

When nature gives us so many things and ultimately nature flourish itself more.

In the same way it teaches us to give love and happiness to each other and grow and evolve from within to achieve a sense of peace and calm inside us.

Evolve as a human being also because it creates a self conscious mind that allow us to connect with ourselves and make us realize that what we want from our life.

So apart from growing as a human being and improving day by day in skills, it is important to take a break from your daily chores and enjoy your surroundings.

Do whatever you can, whatever hobbies you like, trekking playing any kind of sport, sometimes party with friends.

These small things will give you a break and will realign you to focus again.

I think spending time in nature or doing those things which nourish your soul and bring positivity really influence someone's life.

So make a habit of taking breaks also.

Apart from your Goal your life is also important.

Live your life as well.

The boy just had attempted his exam and now its turn to just wait for the results again.

He was passing his days by tooking adventurous trips and spending time with his family.

He reclined his mind on a break and ultimately passes his days in a calm manner.

Everything can be solved with a calm manner.

It just need a practice to achieve that calmness stage.

Days have passed and the boy was waiting for the results.

Only few days were left for the results to be declared.

Somehow the boy managed to calm his senses and realign his focus on his daily chores.

To control your emotions should be your biggest strategy because when a person loses their emotions then anybody has the power to manipulate them.

So work on that also.

One of the important thing in learning is to have fun.

Just have fun in the process of learning.

Don't feel stressed or feel burden in your learning process.

Just have fun and enjoy the process of learning.

There should be a flow in your work.

When you seem that you are enjoying and time passes away as you are working, then just understood that this is your real passion. Because when you are not watching the time while doing work then the result would be automatically positive.

Finally the time arrived of the result and the boy checked his result and somehow when he checked he was just not surprised but happy also because his hard work finally paid off.

Yes he was selected and qualified for his exam with the best rank.

He burst into joy with his family.

Sometimes family seems more happier then you because your achievement is their achievement.

When he got selected with the best rank then he understood and realized the power of not giving up and try even more harder than the before.

So not giving up will give you the positive result one day.

Just believe in yourself and focus on your goal.

When your purpose seems bigger than your fear then nobody can stop you.

Fear always steps human backwards in their field of progress.

So cease your fear and start chasing your purpose.

Purpose comes from exploring yourself and building yourself.

Work on yourself till you become a star.

Keep working on you until your inner child becomes proud of you that you did it.

Learning should be your constant process.

Don't stop learning if you get on your target.

Just keep learning and explore yourself even more to achieve higher goals.

Don't stop on your first target rather than keep exploring yourself and keep learning.

When we keep learning we evolve not as a human being also but also in a goal term also.

Always try to see life from everyone perspective of view.

Everyone has a different meaning of life.

You can learn from everyone.

There is something to learn from each individual.

All have unique capabilities, so try to learn different things from them whether its about life or about any field.

Don't judge them rather than learn from them.

Each individual has unique capabilities to offer this world.

So sit with them, it will expand your growth.

When the boy finally got selected he was happy not because he got selected but because he trusted his journey and he never gave up on his dreams.

He tried his best.

He learnt all the phases of his journey and he realized that it expanded his growth.

He finally entered into a new chapter of his life and now he is ready to climb the stairs and make more opportunities like this.

When you want to be a star just keep evolving and growing in every phase of your life.

Surely you will be a star.

So this was the story of the boy who didn't give up on his dreams and tried his best to achieve his Goal.

When you truly want something then nobody can stop you from getting there.

You just have to start and the way appears.

When you go on the way then you will find many obstacles and hurdles in your path.

These challenges will grow you as a human being and will get you ready for your next level of success.

So always be ready for challenges. Whatever you get enter in any phase of your life, you learn something new everyday.

Try new things everyday, it will make you explore yourself and will make you feel aware to yourself.

Start doing things that are new to u and grow from it, whether you can't do it or the diffulties that came in front of you, just learn from the lessons and eventually you will grow from it.

Make yourself a priority and life will reward you with so many things.

Just trust the Universe and yourself.

What you feel about yourself Universe will send you exact same thing.

Start believing that you are capable of achieving new things.

When you start believing you will attract according to it.

It all starts with you, how you are strongly determined towards your Goals.

Just stay firm to it and act according to it.

When any obstacle come towards your Goal don't get disappointed, instead learn and grow from it.

Many things that are obstacle to you are making you strong and bold person.

So there is a belief that if you are confident in yourself and honest with your dreams and honestly you work for it then nobody can stop you.

Just start manifesting of what you desire.

There are many desires in our lives, some get manifest while some of them we grow from it.

Don't get scared of doing things, just get excited to new things and new adventures.

Life is full of adventures and many adventures serves many purpose into our lives.

These purposes will eventually make us a better human being.

Just do those things which you are at best and the work which bring fun into your life.

Don't rush towards the crowd, just rush towards your passion.

When you follow your passion then automatically success will follow you.

Don't think that my passion is small or it has no value, if you are best in your work and bring happiness to it then that work is hundred percent right to you.

Follow your passion and Goals.

Don't get stressed that things are not going according to you.

Some things don't go according to us.

Because life is meant to teach you something from it.

So if some things are not according to you, so don't get disappointed, instead smile and learn from it.

Learning should be a phase of your life.

Learn from each chapter of you life.

Every chapter serve purpose to build us.

They shape us to a grown human being.

It all starts with your mind.

When you think things are possible it will work out.

It is just a state of your mind.

Your mindset will develop you.

So if your mindset is strong enough to achieve your Goals, then you will certainly will.

So start developing your mindset.

When your mindset is strong then you are capable of achieving higher things into your life.

So build your mindset and sit with those people whose mindset is strong.

It will inspire you to achieve your Goals.

Start practicing gratitude into your life.

When you practice gratitude then life will reward you with so many things.

Life only give those things to people who are gratitude and grateful to their life.

When you are grateful towards your life, then automatically you start attracting new things.

Be humble and start your Goal by doing small things into your life.

These small things will eventually will bring towards your Goal.

Do your own thing and trust the process and enjoy the journey of your dream life.

Start sitting with mindful people who have certain Goals.

Surround yourself to those people who inspire you and bring the best from you.

Start meeting new people in your life.

Each person has certain thing by which we can learn from it.

Learn from each human being because each person has something to offer to this world.

Greet people with your infectious smile.

Because what you give, you will attract.

Learn from your mistakes and from your experiences.

Start developing mindful habits that will sharpen your mind and make you sharp.

Train your brain to do healthier habits.

Train your brain by doing mindful activities.

When you train your brain you can handle the pressures of your life.

Most people get depressed because eventually they are very sensitive to certain things.

When we train our mind to act firmly to any situation, then nobody can make us feel broke.

So stat doing mindful activities.

While developing your mindset, start having healthy items into your diet.

With mental fitness, physical fitness is also necessary.

Do workouts.

Move your body.

Do anything that will bring to your own soul.

Some things like meditation, yoga, Dance, aerobics.

Whatever you do, just move your body and ultimately it will reward you.

Start making your Garden and the butterflies will attract. So the map of your life is based on your mindset.

When your mindset is strong enough then you can achieve anything.

Mindset don't born naturally.

You have to develop it.

Mindset can be develop by adapting healthy habits and choosing people who are good for your mental health.

Choose people who push you to be better day by day.

Make a daily routine and stick to it.

Consistency and discipline will lead you towards your success.

Discipline is very important for building your success.

When you are discipline enough you will stick to your daily routine.

Motivation will not drive you to success but discipline will drive you to success.

Stay committed to your Goals.

When you are committed to certain thing whether your diet plan, your skin routine, your fitness routine, it will improve day by day.

Just find your passion and stick to it and improve it day by day.

When you work on your passion, then you work on your success.

You can identify your passion by exploring yourself.

Explore new things and identify that at which thing you are at best.

The thing that bring you fun and you enjoy doing that thing, that is your passion.

When you work on your passion then you don't have to force anything.

Your natural talent will flow and you will enjoy the process.

Time will flow smoothly while working on your passion.

Just make tiny steps towards your Goal and enjoy the process.

So if you have to do something big then start with small and stick to that plan.

Certainly these things will guide you towards your Goal.

To accomplish your Goal believe in yourself that you can do it.

If you will believe then you will manifest.

It all starts with you.

When you will believe in yourself then everyone else will believe you.

Manifestation begins in believers.

Those who believe will ignite the flame of their dreams.

Sometimes you get doubts that whether you will do it or not.

But you have to hold the grip that you will achieve it.

When you start taking positive affirmations then magical things happen.

Things get to those who don't give up and believe in themselves.

So start taking positive affirmations.

While achieving your Goal, live your life also because passing time will not come again.

Explore your hobbies and make time for your hobbies that freshen up your mood and charge you.

Travel to new places, try different adventures in your life.

Meet new people and learn their ideas and beliefs.

Meeting new people will give you many new ideas that will help you grow.

So start meeting with new people.

Start welcoming new changes.

When you start giving time to yourself then you start giving time to your dreams.

Just start focusing on yourself.

Focus on your health, on your life, on your dreams and you will surely achieve height of your dreams.

You will fall many times but get up and refuse to give up on your dreams.

Try many times as you can because one day you will be proud that you didn't give up.

Build your healthy habits.

Future is great of those who have healthy habits.

By practicing gratitude and enjoying the process, you will certainly go ahead in your life.

Learn from your mistakes and don't repeat them.

It's ok to commit mistakes but to repeat it is not ok.

Try to learn from the failures and admire your journey.

These ups and downs will certainly will be fruitful to you.

Just stay committed towards your Goals.

When we accomplish one thing then there is inner confidence that we can achieve next thing also.

Just start picking up your small Goals and try to accomplish them.

When you set your small Goals and you accomplish them, you will certainly achieve your higher Goals.

Don't just imagine your future but act also according to it.

Set the target and complete it.

When you set your small target you are setting your big target.

Higher Goals need higher energy.

For higher energy to be obtained, you have to take care of yourself, mentally and physically.

Health is wealth

So start prioritizing your health.

Eat nutritious food, get plenty of sleep, socialize to good people who bring the best in you.

Start setting boundaries and start believing more in yourself.

Be kind to people.

Do good things that bring peace to your soul.

Have mindful conversations that increase your productivity.

Make time for your hobbies.

Beside having your Goals, party harder because your time will not come back.

Enjoy the small moments and cherish the moments of your life.

Watch sunset.

Do crazy things that bring the inner kid.

Do things that bring you alive.

Being alive is a special occasion.

When you start living your life, you will certainly feel good.

Be happy, be you.

Sometimes situation might not go according to us.

But don't panic.

Just go with the flow and reassure yourself that this is the part to learn something.

Learn from new adventures of your life.

Learn each day new everything.

Each day serves a purpose to learn.

Learn from the experiences and from your life decisions.

Don't judge yourself that you took a decision wrong, instead learn from them that how can you not repeat this mistake again.

We are human beings, we make mistakes.

To do a mistake is a good thing but to repeat them is not a good thing.

So learn from your mistakes and visualize them that where you went wrong and how you can correct them.

Learning should be your part of your growth phase.

Don't stop learning.

Learn new skills, new activities that bring purpose to your life.

Enjoy the little things in your life.

If you are at peace with yourself, then nothing can disturb you.

Happiness comes from inside, not from materialistic things.

If you are happy and satisfied with your inner being then nothing can stop you.

Always make yourself and your happiness a priority.

When you will prioritize yourself then everything will be according to you.

Give your hundred percent to your all tasks.

Focus is the main factor.

Most people don't achieve things because their focus is poor.

If average student focus is sharp then that person will surely achieve his dreams.

Build your focus and your actions will be superb.

Focus can be aligned by various methods.

By deep meditation.

By focusing on a single task.

Don't do multitask it will decrease your focus and you can't be do anything right.

Do a single task efficiently.

In between your work give yourself a break times.

In five to ten minutes of break you can do anything like listening to music, or having a nap.

Just do what is suitable for you.

Having your sharp focus will align you to at your right work.

Right focus requires a much practice and patience.

It requires true honesty from yourself.

Whatever work you do be honest with it.

When you are honest with yourself and with your work, your work would be perfect.

Once you develop your right focus then you can develop the right strategy to do it.

So begin with a smile a develop a high focus.

Sharp focus can built over a months or in years.

It requires how much you practice and how you stick to it.

Just choose one task and finish it without distracting.

Before starting a work, meditate for a while to improve focus.

When you meditate your focus will improve and your work will flow.

Apart from deep focus relax for a while.

Don't get stressed that what will happen if this might not work.

Just relax and inhale and exhale and trust the journey and enjoy the process.

When you enjoy the process then work will be efficiently improve.

So do it in a relaxed manner and be positive that I will give my hundred percent to my work.

You can achieve anything by immense focus and with positive energy.

It all starts with you and with your goals that how much you are committed to them.

When everything seems tired, give a pause and take a break and relax for a while.

Giving up is not a solution, if you want truly something then try harder and harder till you succeed.

When you will not give up and see how far you have come then you will thank yourself for not giving up.

This will show that how strong is your mindset is.

Achieving one goal will boost your confidence and give you more confidence to achieve more and to have more dreams.

Just start with tiny step and complete your small Goal.

Trust your journey and have faith in yourself that whatever you will do will be with hundred percent focus and you will proudly say one day that you did it.

Making yourself your inner kid proud should be your highest Goal.

Make your inner kid proud.

Love yourself.

Take care of yourself.

Grow from within. When your mindset is in growth stage, then any difficult situation you can overcome.

When you have shape your mind to overcome from any hurdle and obstacle, you are making the way for success.

So first assume success in your mind then automatically you will perform in a wonderful manner.

Help the needy people, it will keep you grounded.

Make yourself happy by finding joy in little things.

Hold on to things and people which make you smile.

Spend time with people with whom you feel good and cherish the moments with them.

Life is such a beautiful gift.

Enjoy the moments and live your life also.

Go for hiking, climb the mountain, do your hobbies that bring a smile on your face.

We have given this beautiful life so spend it wisely.

Walk in nature. Explore yourself.

Go on solo trips and enjoy the little precious moments that make you feel alive.

Do craziest things like paintings, playing any instrument.

These activities will sharpen your mind and broaden your perspective.

Spend your precious time with those people who lit up your life and bring happiness and pushes you to be a better human being.

Collect those moments and memories and when you will recall these moments then you will smile that these were the days you were living for.

Live your life personally and professionally.

Don't mix them two.

Make a balance between these two and you will have a balanced life.

When you will be discipline and honest with yourself and with your life then life will reward you with extraordinary things.

Just stay consistent.

When we are open minded and change our thoughts according to the generation, then new generation will also accept us.

Change with the time.

Keep your morals and beliefs old but see new things as new perspectives.

Understand the different perspective of human beings.

All human beings are different.

Understand all their perspectives also.

Everyone have some unique qualities.

Try to understand them and create new ideas from all human beings.

Listen to their ideas and narrate your ideas also.

Go with the team.

When you will grow together you will win.

If you want to go far go together.

Convert your weakness into strength.

If you have any weakness, don't cry that why I have got this, instead convert them into your strength.

Be bold and strong that one day whatever the today's circumstances are you will eventually win if you never give up.

So smile and get ready to face the challenges.

Challenges are your part of your growth.

When you don't fear your challenges then your fears will run away.

Face your fears and challenges.

These challenges will make you a strong person.

One day you will be proud that you have overcome your challenges.

Challenges make you believe that how capable you are.

Our capabilities arises when storm comes.

We broke, we cry but we get up and come up stronger.

So whenever new challenges come, just smile that these challenges will build a pathway for your growth.

Grow from each aspect of your life.

Growth is necessary if you want to achieve something.

Face your fears and difficulties.

Do challenges task, it will embrace your growth.

After some difficult task if you experience pain, then it's a sign of growth and magical things are about to happen.

Where there is pain, there is gain.

So if you are experiencing pain in something then life will reward you with sweetness.

So taste bitter now, and have sweet later.

Pain of discipline is better then pain of regret.

When any person scold you fro your mistakes then it will improve you.

Similarly if someone pat you on your back for your mistakes, then later it would be difficult for you to change.

Adapt to your new surroundings.

Adaptation is the law of the nature. Whatever the circumstances are try to adapt.

Don't get panic that how will you deal with these changes.

Instead try to adjust with them with your growth mindset.

That's why growth mindset is important.

It helps you to your changing environment.

When your mindset will grow you will cross all the hurdles of your life.

So Adaptation is the new key for the growth.

Be ready for any changes in your life.

Life is not fair sometimes.

You may deal with many situations where you can't expect that this might happen.

So embrace the changes and see life from a different perspective.

Embrace changes but don't lose yourself.

Be yourself no matter what, but grow from all things, whether from experiences, from your environment.

Ready to change.

So you see there are many factors which will drive you to the road of success.

But to achieve that success you don't have to be excellent.

You just need sharp focus, discipline and consistency.

When you develop these habits then you will flow to the road of success.

So build these characteristics and include them in your life.

When you will develop these then you will feel inner peace and well being in your inner soul.

Just try out these habit if you want to grow your career.

Success is a marathon. Not a sprint.

Discipline and determination are your running shoes.

No one is going to go out of their way to tell you this but you can create anything you want if you make it a priority.

So start focusing on your Goals.

When you focus on the good, good things happen.

When you focus on the problems, more problems get created.

Try to find the solution of everything.

Great leaders find solutions in everything.

If you want to be a leader, work with the team.

Go with the team and work as a team.

The leader support their team.

Leader listens to them and work according to all the perspectives of mind of the people.

They find solutions and don't panic.

They create the solutions of the problems and cheer for their team.

Good leader is supportive and a listener.

They make decisions that are good for the team.

They listen to each person and work according to them.

They correct the flaws and their decision making power is very strong.

Leaders are bold and have empathy towards others.

Emotional intelligence plays a crucial role in the development of success.

If you are emotional mature and have empathy towards each human being then you create great connections and form a stronger bond with others.

When you understand the sufferings of human beings you understand their emotions.

Emotional intelligence make you a good human being and a good leader.

As a leader you understand the need of others and work according to them.

When you develop emotional intelligence you develop patience and you support and listen empathetically.

A person who wants to build a business if develop emotional intelligence then that person business will grow tremendously.

So having empathy is good for your future career.

The persons who have empathy are naturally humble.

When you are aware of your emotions, you can control them.

If you know your weakness then you can make it to your strength.

So if you are aware that what you are feeling then you can simply counter them and control it.

If you know the emotions then you can judge that whether the person is actually angry or the person is wounded.

Emotional intelligence develops great communication skills.

Your listening power is good if you have empathy.

When you listen to other people ideas then you can judge that whether to continue this communication or not.

If you are doing any business, and your listening capacity is good then you can make good investments.

You can have a high profit if you have good communication skills.

It makes you a good human being and a humble person.

Apart from emotional intelligence, good communication skills also serve benefit to your career.

If you have good communication skills then you can master great deals.

Good communication skills also need practice.

Try to communicate daily.

Meet with new person daily communicate with them at any topic.

It will boost your confidence and increase your self esteem.

Such type of qualities need practice and patience.

Now we come to empathy.

Empathy can be generated since childhood.

When the kids are small, just give them a pet either kitten or dog.

They learn that how to form bonds and they develop empathy towards them.

When they develop empathy, they become human beings.

Firstly become a human being.

Feel the emotions but don't be emotional.

There is a difference between being emotional and having emotional intelligence.

Emotional intelligence means to become aware of the emotions while emotional means you feel the things deeply.

When you become emotional then you can't judge what is good or bad.

You just get fooled away by emotions.

But if you develop emotional intelligence, then you are aware that what the person is actually feeling.

So be aware of these two situations.

Try to observe things rather than absorbing them.

When you observe things then you are developing a good sense of observing power.

Observe your surroundings that what is happening.

Don't get indulge in it.

If any negative thing is happening, then observe it rather than absorbing it.

Observation makes you intelligent and more focused individual.

So practice to observe.

The most powerful tool you can use is your senses.

When you observe with your senses about good and bad things, you become aware of this world.

Life is full of colors.

Try to identify these colors that which colors you want to include them in your life.

There are good and bad colors.

So its up to you that which colors you adopt to your life.

Choosing those colors will decide your future.

Choosing colors means that which type of habits you want to adopt in life.

Now if you have reached mental fitness, now physical fitness is also necessary.

Train your body to be physically fit.

Have protein rich diet.

Hit the gym.

Move your body.

When you are physically healthy from inside then you will do amazing things.

Physical fitness will give you so many opportunities to perform.

Everything requires hard work.

If you are willing to want something, then you have to pay for that.

Nothing comes free.

The higher the ambition, the higher will be the price.

Sacrifices comes with hard work.

Get ready to sacrifice things for your dreams.

If you feel pain in your dreams while working for it then you are in the right direction.

New beginnings requires many goodbyes.

Be ready to say goodbye to many things that hinders your growth and your potential.

Sit with people who are above you in experiences, in terms of growth, in terms of money.

When you sit with these kind of people, your life will level up.

Start recognizing such type of people and make connections with them.

To become a butterfly you have to go through many phases.

In each phase your growth should be increased.

When your potential get sharper day by day you will feel more confident.

So start having friendships to such type of people.

When you are confident enough to believe in your dreams then you can manifest it also.

It all starts with you and your dreams that how much you are passionate about your dreams and how bold you are to take action for it.

When you see and dream, first manifest in your mind that you can do it.

Plan according to it and then execute it.

Execution is more important than your ideas.

When your execution is right your path would also be right.

Have faith that everything would work out.

If you have faith in yourself and in your God then nothing is impossible.

Just take the risk and do it.

Do it for yourself.

Don't do it for anyone rather than do it for yourself that what will you get after this.

Would you be happy or satisfied after doing your work.

Just trust it and make a jump.

When everything seems come to halt, just take a break.

Don't quit.

If you have seen any dream then you have the power to manifest it.

Just keep honesty with yourself, that whatever you will do will be hundred percent by your side, then your life will get changes.

Just keep believing and enjoy your life.

Life only comes ones.

Just enjoy this beautiful life and capture all the moments of your life whether good or bad.

Good moments will give you happiness while bad moments will give you lessons that you don't have to repeat this mistake again.

Life is all about experiences and lessons.

When you will focus on the grief, grief will grow but if you will focus on the lesson you will grow as a human being.

So grow from each and everything.

Life should not be stop.

It has to be move on.

So if you will smile, life will smile you back.

What you give to this universe, you will get.

Get the sunlight.

Step outside.

There is so much to experience in life.

Experience from each phase of your life.

Enjoy this life.

Don't fear that what might happen in this phase.

Just get excited about the task and focus on your beautiful journey.

When you will smile, people would gather around you by seeing your infectious energy.

Greet people, wish them from your heart.

When you will do such genuine things, genuine people would attract towards you.

Make your life a joyful thing.

Spread joy wherever you go.

Spread kindness.

These small gestures will impact a many person's lives.

Your life will also get improve and your surrounded people would also feel well.

Make your environment happy and joyful.

Environment plays a huge role in everyone's lives.

Choose your environment carefully.

When you will choose people right, your life would also be joyful.

Make a large connection of good people who will help you whenever you need.

When there is a strong network, your growth occurs not just financially but also in all phases of life.

When you get up from the bed, then do that thing which bring positive energy to your life.

You can do whatever thing you like, as meditation, reading a book.

So this is all about manifestation and how you can deal when you are tired and thinking to quit.

Now there is a one story also.

So lets begin.

There was a Boy who always use to complain about his life, about his situations.

Whenever life throws any challenge to him, he grew frustrated and always complaining that this should not be happen to him.

In this way his mindset get narrower day by day, he couldn't think what is right and what is wrong.

Then he met a boy of his age, he had nothing in his life, no family, no home to live, he lived in a tent nearby.

But he was willing to do hard work for his dreams.

He wanted to be a Doctor.

Despite all these situations, he study till late at night so that he could get a good college.

He was practicing gratitude that whatever he has, sufficient for him.

Now he will work hard more to achieve all those things that he deserve.

So its all in the mindset that how we perceive things and how we apply those things in our life.

It's the focused mind and determination that led to the path of self discovery and success.

So its up to you that which path you want to go.

Either go in the direction of gratitude, or go in the direction of complaing always.

When you will choose gratitude, life will reward you with so many things that you can't even think.

So choose gratitude everyday and you will shine one day.

When the boy who saw this tent boy who had nothing but gratitude, he also began to think that I can also change my life by showing gratitude.

Gratitude always changes our lives.

Its magical.

There is so much to smile, that we forget in our sorrows.

Life is such a beautiful gift that is given to us.

Appreciate this life, grow in life.

When the boy started choosing gratitude, his whole story changes.

He began to smile more, his decision making power also gets improve.

His mind become calm.

He began to see things clearly.

That's the power of gratitude.

He started visualizing success in his mind and began to work for it.

What you can dream, you can achieve.

If you constantly keep saying good things to you, then good things also happen to you.

What you think, you become.

He shaped his career on the basis of his thinking.

When your mindset is strong enough then you can achieve higher things in your life.

Build your mindset and you will get ahead in life.

When the world is against you but you have the power to not give up, then nobody can stop you.

Its you vs you.

You are your own competitor.

Just make sure that you are on the higher level than your previous day.

The boy make sure not to complain rather to learn each day.

When you improve yourself and your habits, then there is increment in your growth.

Start showing real honesty to your work, to yourself.

Start investing in yourself.

Overall a month the boy performance get advanced and he was visualizing dreams of his own and was working upon them.

When you suddenly get distracted, just look into the lives of those that inspire you, that have nothing but are trying each day to get better.

Life is full of ups and downs.

When you start visualizing dreams, then it will come up in the forms of up and downs.

You have to be humble when life is getting smoother, when life gets tough you have to be strong to face those challenges.

Life is not fair sometimes.

You have to make it.

Its all in your mindset and your daily habits that will make your life.

So start manifesting and create abundance opportunities in your life.

Opportunities comes to us in many forms.

Either we create them or don't miss those opportunities.

Some opportunities we miss either due to our shyness or due to our comfort zone.

But try to chase those opportunities, because these opportunities will build your life and will create better growth for you.

First time it would be uncomfortable to you, but you will get addicted to it if you start chasing those opportunities.

So start working on yourself.

When we are ready for any opportunity then we create better choices in our life.

Don't do it for anyone but for yourself.

When you do better choices for yourself, better results will come and better growth will also occur.

So start manifesting your dreams.

Do it with small and you will eventually grow big.

It's all in the mindset that what you are filling inside.

So when you are bold enough to chase your dreams then nobody can stop you.

When we are true to ourselves, then we are true to others.

First start being true to yourself.

When you are consistently being committed to your Goals and dreams then nothing can stop you.

Stay true to means that you are willing to do hard work and whatever is required to achieve them, you will claim it if you are hundred percent stay committed towards your Goals.

So expect everything from yourself, and you will live a wonderful life.

When you are willing to give everything to your Dreams, you will never regret that why I didn't invest time in myself.

Insecurities will come, but you have to show up every time towards your work.

When you will develop enough self confidence to achieve them, then it doesn't matter that what the outside circumstances are.

At the end you will shine when your hard work will come outside.

So stay committed towards your Goals.

When you attained peace and success then life ultimately Goal is to create more opportunities in your life.

If you want to be on top then just don't stop where you are but keep chasing more great things that bring ultimately joy to your life.

When you will chase greater things, you will become great person.

You have to choose that what you want to bring on your table, either greatness or pain of regret.

We always think in life that we should do this but our actions define our life and personality.

Our actions should be matched with our words.

Our actions define that who we are.

So build the habits that bring good actions into your life.

Stay committed to your words that will bring good fortune to your life.

Do that work that bring immense joy and peace to your life.

In the end satisfaction will ensure you that what you did was great.

When we are not sure that where we should go in life and what actions should we take, that wherever we are going in a right direction.

Just ask yourself that is this work bringing joy and satisfaction to your life.

If you are satisfied with your work then what you are doing is right and you should come forward to do great things in your life in the area of your work.

When we keep trying hard and pursue our passions then our passion becomes our destiny.

Make your passion your destiny.

You can create your destiny by working hard and following your passion.

When we are willing to take risk then success will follow you.

Those who are not afraid of taking risks are the real one heroes.

Develop your strategy of your work that can bring real growth in your life.

Real growth starts when you are willing to take risks and you are honest with your dreams and with your life.

So act according to it.

When you will act, you growth will be seen to everyone.

Now comes the focus part.

When you are focus and you are in right alignment then nobody can stop you reaching your target.

So deep focus is very necessary.

Deep focus requires many methods and strategies to build your life.

Deep focus comes from practice.

Just start your practice with the small steps.

When you will practice for a short time then increase your practice time to maintain your habit.

Deep focus is a habit and you have to cultivate it.

With deep focus an average person can go into excellent stage where if a focus is poor then a excellent person can't achieve his dreams.

So build your focus and you will get ahead in life.

Its all about the right and deep focus which you have to cultivate it to build your dreams.

To build deep focus you have to not be distracted by the things that are hampering in your work.

Just do meditation before starting any work.

Remove all the distractions from your work table and just do your work without distracting.

Initially you will distract but after sometimes your focus will improve and you will be in right alignment.

Deep focus requires lots of practice and patience.

When you are patience with yourself then you are patience with your work.

So keep it slow but improve day by day.

When you have your healthy diet and you are consistent with your work then you are honest with your work.

It all starts with you that how you deal with the situations of your daily life and how you face those challenges.

Ultimately your character would develop when you are honest with your work.

So build your focus and get aligned to your work.

Just make a to do list that what you have to do throughout day and when you will see that you have completed your list then there is a inner satisfaction that you did your best on your day.

Don't think about the future or your destination.

Rather think about the present day that what you have to do throughout your day to bring the best.

When your day is successful then your years would be successful.

Just think about the present moment and you will reach your destination.

Your ultimately goal should be that how can you make your present moment best.

When you want to do the things of your routine.

Do hard things first.

The things which are hard will make you feel lighter that you did your hard work.

So choose hard and do this task first.

Sometimes life give you lemons, so make a creative side of that.

There are so many things which we can create in our own life.

You just have to observe that what kind of things are present around me and build a beautiful thing of that.

When you create beautiful things, and cherish the good moments in your life then you will see new magic that will occur in your life.

Trust the timing of your life.

Everything will come to you at the exact moment.

You get what you planted.

So plant a beautiful garden and butterflies will chase in your garden.

Cultivate good flowers in your garden and your garden would give so much fragrance.

When you are willing to do hard work and you makeup your mind that at anyhow I have to perform well not just in my work but as a human being also.

When such mindset you develop, whatever the circumstances are, you will handle it and in the end you will proudly say that things get happen and you didn't give up.

You just need a little bit patience and confidence to achieve your dreams.

Just each day say to yourself that you can do it and you will.

.When we are willing to take risk and go further beyond our fears then magical things happen.

We are willing to take risk when there is no fear about anything that what might happen and if it doesn't work out.

So always go beyond your fears.

When there is no fear, there is a winning side.

If you couldn't win then you might learn something.

Learning should be your first priority.

When we learn daily, then we grow daily.

Learning is a part of success.

What we always assume might not be correct. Sometimes we doubt our potential but we all are made up of magic.

Magic is hidden in all of us.

We have to discover it on the based of our hobbies.

When we work on our hobbies then our passion arises by working on it.

When we are sure that what we want in our life, just make a strategy and do it.

When you are sure that you have to go in this path, then nothing should come in between.

Just rather apply the plan and do it.

Ride on the boat and do it.

Don't think too much that it will work or not.

When God have given you a vision to dream it then God will help you to achieve it.

Those who are sure that they will make it one day will surely achieve it.

Those who have faith in themselves that one day they will reach their destination despite all the obstacles, they will claim it for sure.

So just go for your dreams and never settle in life because one day your faith will lead you towards your inner level of peace and success.

Whenever we get stuck that what should we do next then explore yourself and regain in your hobby and make it your work.

The work that bring you smile on your face and you seem enjoyable doing it that work is perfect for you.

Don't chase money rather than chase your passion.

Similarly don't chase grades rather than chase knowledge.

When you indulge yourself in your learning process then good things happen to you and you will get good grades.

Just hope for the best that everything will work out.

When you will indulge yourself in your work then everything will work out in your favor.

Just trust your God and your timing that everything will get towards you at correct time.

Life is all about learning process.

Whatever your age is, if you keep learning in life you will always be forward in life.

You will never get old if you keep learning in life.

There are millions of neurons in our Brain.

Learning increases our neurons.

Many diseases occurs as we get old like dementia, Alzheimer's disease but if we get engaged in using our Brain then our brain and mind will be young.

Our brain capacity get increases if we indulge in these type of activities.

So indulge in meditation, involving in any skill like playing piano or Guitar.

Just do these type of activities and you will see the results.

These all activities will become a part of your life when you get these habits in your daily life.

Our brain get addicted to things which we form a habit either bad or good.

So its up to you that which type of habit you want to adapt in life.

In beginning the habits would be boring but eventually your brain will need it at that exact time.

It's the part of the normal brain process.

So eat healthy foods, include protein in your diet, have sunlight that nourishes your Brain.

Comfort zone is a very beautiful zone in which every person want to stay.

But you have to move from your comfort zone to grow.

When we leave our comfort zone then our real growth starts.

Growth is painful.

To be consistent in growth, one must be have to be very patient to himself.

When you are patient with yourself and with your work, then there will be easiness to your growth.

Don't be so hard on yourself.

Take a breaks sometimes to refresh yourself.

Just divide the time according to your priority.

You are a human, not a machine.

Give less time but do your work deeply.

When you do your work with deep focus, then anything is possible.

Deep focus is very important for your work.

An average person get excellent in many things if focus is great.

Develop this habit of deep focus to get right alignment in your work and in your Goals.

Sometimes in life, many things are not control within us.

When many things which are not under control, leave them as it is and get flow with it.

When we flow with the things then naturally our stress reduced and some things are under control.

Get flow with the things, which you can not understand.

You will get huge peace after doing this.

Just get flow with it and do your work.

Some things are very simple in life, we just complicate them by overthinking.

Life is simple, just live your life and do the things that make you happy.

When you are happy then you can take the decisions clearly in life.

Don't take the decisions of your life when you are angry.

In angry situations we often make mistakes.

When you are in a elite mood then take the decisions.

That decisions will be best decisions of your life.

Try to make yourself peaceful and calm throughout the journey.

When you are in a calm mood then everything becomes joyful.

So always try to be calm in every situations.

Control your emotions every time, don't get too emotional at everything.

When you get too emotional then chances of manipulation are higher.

Live your life beautifully.

Have purpose in life and work for it.

Everyone serves purpose to this land.

Find your purpose and work for it.

Life is a journey that have ups and downs.

No life is straight.

You will have many experiences in life some are good, some are bad.

Good experiences will give you memories and bad experiences will give you lessons to grow in life.

Life is full of sweet and bitterness.

Both are essential in life to build your career.

You can't expect always positive things in life.

Every season serves a purpose.

Enjoy every season of your life.

When we smile through the challenges then challenges seems easier to handle.

So grow from each season and build your life.

Have faith that everything would work out.

Don't compare your life to anyone.

No one is superior nor inferior.

You are You.

I am I.

Your competition is only you.

Start having positive talks with yourself.

How you treat yourself and how you talk with yourself really matters.

When you treat yourself good then you allow others to treat you good.

So it all starts with you.

Having a healthy mindset, having healthy boundaries and maintaining good connections happen when you treat yourself good and you are honest with yourself.

Every time you do yourself good, treat yourself with reward, either go for a trip or party with friends.

Keep your close friends close to you that bring best in you and keep you motivated to do better in life.

Make sure you are surrounded with such type of people that bring the best in you.

When you feel motivated then such type of friends will make you ensure that you are doing well in life.

So find these true friends.

First make yourself your best friend.

When you know yourself well then you can know your feelings that why you are feeling this way.

When you exactly know that what you want in life.

When you exactly know yourself then you work according to it.

You work hard and improve yourself day by day.

When you know your weakness, you make it to your strength.

Keep pursuing your dreams and keep shining.

When you are sure about your life that what you want to do and how you want to spend your days, then it brings clarity.

Clarity comes when you spend time with yourself.

Spending time with yourself will allow your inner thoughts to come and you begin to think clear.

Always make time for yourself for a while.

It is important to have a conversation with yourself.

One day all these struggles and hard work, would be grateful to you.

You will smile that you didn't give up.

Cherish your life and life will reward you with so many things.

When you are consistent with your life, and with your dreams then your destination of your dreams is sure.

Just stay consistent and never give up.

Take a break from your life but if you want truly something and if it is not working, don't change the destination rather than change the plan.

When you truly want something then you have to work hard for it to achieve your dream life.

Just admire your life, when you praise yourself in your little things that how far you have come, how you constantly try each day to become best.

When you admire yourself and your life, then life would certainly reward you with so many things in life.

Just keep showing gratitude each day and you will see the magic of gratitude.

When little things make you happy and you find joy in little things, that where your actual happiness starts.

Happiness is found in little things in our life.

You just have to switch the bulb of happiness.

When life reward you either with praise or with lessons just keep them both and show gratitude that one day you will try your best to become your best.

When you become the best version of yourself then you are actually happy with yourself because there is inner satisfaction that you did your best.

When you give your best then you feel calm that you gave your hundred percent.

What might didn't happen was the luck.

So next time you don't repeat that mistakes that you have performed in previous attempt.

When you are regular and consistent at your work then you are honest with your work.

Keep showing this honesty to build your life.

Honesty with your work and with your life is your best honesty.

When you are willing to do work and show your work everyday then your work would be admire by all.

Next is to establish and to be permanent consistent with your work you have to make your mindset that one day this consistency will lead you towards your growth.

Whatever is your work, you have to decide your purpose.

Purpose will never let you quit.

Have purpose in your life.

When you are grounded to your work, then your work will be shown by all.

Just do it with small steps and you will get ahead in life.

When you are passionate about your work, then you will not have to be hard daily at your work.

Just consistency and your commitment towards your work will be sufficient enough to be a beast.

Don't be a Rabbit, but be a tortoise.

Slow and steady wins the race.

When you are good enough at your work and you are so much passionate about your work, then nobody can stop you to get ahead in life.

Build extra habits also like discipline, confidence, determination at your work.

These small habits will lead you towards your Goal.

Confidence is not born, it is developed and practice.

When you don't compare to yourself to anyone and you feel safe as you are a person, it is built according to it.

So practice confidence and always ready to face challenges in your life.

When you face challenges in your life, then your perspective will grow as a person.

Start chasing your Goals and make your vision smart and see the world and understand the world from all the perspective view of other people.

When we are happy and satisfied of what we have then we are already rich.

Start showing gratitude of what you have.

Don't worry so much that you can't manifest this or that instead start showing happiness that you have roof over your head, food on your table, have family to love, friends to celebrate your joys and sorrows.

When you start showing value to these things then you are further rich than you can imagine.

And work for your dreams while showing gratitude to these things.

Life is itself a Gift.

When you are fully focused in your life then you are heading towards your milestone.

Another level to define yourself is to include your hobbies.

You need three hobbies to level up your life.

One hobby to create money.

One hobby to be fit.

One hobby to gain knowledge.

When you include these hobbies in to your life, then are leveling up.

Make sure that your time is utilized and to enjoy your life as well.

Your life only comes once.

So don't waste it.

Either enjoy your life or make your life or by balancing both.

It's your life.

Decide for yourself.

To develop money you should be depend on multiple streams.

Because you don't know that when your one source of income will get go.

So be reliable on different streams of income.

Don't just depend on one thing rather than depend on many factors.

Same depend on friendships.

Make different connections of friendship.

One day you don't know that which friend you will need in any situation.

Make good connections of network.

When you entered in any relationship, then don't cutoff your friends because if that relationship get ended then you have good friends to cheer you up.

Always admire yourself, your life, your family.

More you Admire, more you will fulfillish your desires.

You are the constant in your life.

Everything is temporary.

But you are the constant, so work on yourself more.

The more work you will do for yourself, the more productive your life will be.

When you get surrounded by productive people in your life, then there is encouragement that you should also do well in life.

The mindset to grow should be same.

When one will get lazy, he will see other that he is doing productive in life.

So he will also try to do more productive work.

Time is very precious in our life.

Our life is measured by our time.

When we appreciate time, then we are ahead in our life.

So prioritize time and value your time because time is very precious.

Time will never come again in your life.

So utilize your time wisely.

Priortize that what is important to you and what you want to consider in your life.

When you prioritize your things then you get right alignment.

Do the hard things first and prioritize your Goals first.

And the rest of things get come after this.

When we utilize our resources correctly and invest in our time in those things which bring clarity to our life and to our dreams is the time that is best utilized by us.

When our time is utilized in important things then our all tasks are almost done.

We feel a sense of relief that we have done our most important task at timely.

When we consider our responsibilities and are serious about our Goals, then we are turning the direction to change our lives in a positive direction.

Have a clear vision and utilize your time.

Get your vision straight like you are targeting something.

When your target is clear that what you want in your life and what is your purpose in life, then Goal becomes simple.

See big dreams because you are the entire ocean in the drop.

You are the whole ocean.

You can achieve anything in life if you want it truly.

So invest wisely that what you wanted in life.

Create smarter moves because smart strategies always work.

When you have reached a certain point of life that you don't want to go further, say to yourself that why you started.

There will be times when you will feel unmotivated that you don't want to do it.

But your discipline will lead you ahead.

Stay consistent with your wishes and dreams.

Stay in touch with your family, with your friends so that you always feel motivated.

Whenever you feel that I should stop, spend some time with your friends those who will lift you up and bring the best in you.

Some things don't meant to happen, let it go such type of things.

When you welcome new things and make those things work for you, then those things will love you also.

There are many phases in our life, some have happy moments, some have sad moments.

Enjoy both type of moments because every moment will teach you something.

Some will build you, strengthen you and make you feel that all these things are equally important in life.

Growth is very necessary in our life.

When we tend to grow and want to grow in life, then our thinking capacity also grows.

Our thinking capacity will determine that how far we can go in life.

If our thinking and actions align with each other then magic happens.

Magic is present in every human being.

You just have to explore yourself and identified that what you are good at.

When you identify your magic, then apply that magic in your life to see abundance.

When you believe in yourself and have faith in yourself that everything will work out and you will achieve your dreams.

Now that's only matter in life that you are with yourself.

Learn to love yourself.

Love your flaws, your hidden talents.

Explore yourself and this beautiful life.

Life is very beautiful.

Don't waste on things that don't matter in your life.

Life is very short.

Spend it with those people who bring the best in you.

Life is full of different colors.

Each color is unique. Each color have equally impact on our lives.

Try to fill your life with each color.

Just like Rainbow, it have seven different colors yet it looks so beautiful because it is a mixture of colors.

As like our life should be of different colors to look beautiful.

Choose your colors wisely.

Which color you want to include in your life depends on your choices.

Choose colors and radiate colors and spread joy in your life and to other people's lives.

Every time when we are true to ourselves and our aspirations then there is something by which our life get in shape.

When we care for ourselves, then we care for this world.

Start prioritizing yourself and you will better this world by your actions.

When something is beautiful you create inside in your heart, you give that beautiful thing to this world.

Whatever you bring the best in you, you give it to world.

So start giving to yourself first.

Start taking care of your health, start taking care of your needs and all your worries will be away.

Life is all about thanksgiving, purpose and serving ourselves and others.

When we serve ourselves with best needs, then we serve this society also with best needs.

You just have to take charge for yourself.

Nobody is going to save you but only you can save yourself.

You can do anything for you if you are consistent enough and courageous enough to chase your dreams.

Just be bold and brave that one day you will make it.

When you decide it to yourself and you prove to yourself that whatever be the circumstances are you are not going to give up.

You don't have to be perfect for this life.

Just Be Real for this world.

Just make sure that you are fitting in your opinions rather than the opinion of society.

You have the power to change yourself and be a better version of yourself.

When you are changing yourself, you are changing the world.

Don't change the world, rather than change yourself and make this world a better place to live.

When you serve yourself from your beautiful actions then your beautiful actions will change the world.

Just make sure that you are giving your best in each attempt.

Make a time for your life also.

Do the things that makes you happy.

Spend time with your loved ones.

Do crazy stuff and do the things that make you believe in yourself.

Move your body, love your body and be kind to yourself and be kind to everyone.

Everyone is fighting their silent battle, you know nothing about.

Beside having a Goal, be a better human being also not just for yourself but for everyone.

Make this world a better place by being yourself.

When you are being yourself, you attract the people in your life who belongs to you.

When you are willing to help yourself, then you are willing to help others.

First help yourself, when you help yourself, you can help the world.

When something is good for you, you can feel it.

Your intuition never lies. When you are surrounded by a negative or positive energy, your intuition identifies it and on the basis of that you get surrounded by people.

So trust your intuition.

Sometimes its better to trust your intuition.

Intuition clarifies the energy.

Begin to identify the energy of the people.

Life is full of happiness and sorrows.

If you will get happiness, then there will be sorrows also.

If there will be no sorrows, then you can't feel the happiness.

So both are equally important.

When there is happiness, share the happiness with others.

And when there is sorrow, have some patience that this phase will pass away soon.

Happiness will give you lot of memories and sorrows will give you lessons.

Everything happens for a real reason in life.

Whatever happens there is a cause behind it.

So don't get panic what have happened, instead try to find a solution of it.

Great leaders find a solution of everything.

When in doubt always find your best abilities and work towards your best abilities to perform well in life.

When you make your qualities even more special, then your qualities will define you.

Make your qualities your identity.

Develop the good habits for your productive life.

When you will develop the good habits or healthy habits that are good to your mind then you will perform well in life.

Just get stick to your habits and the habits will stick to you.

When you will develop these kind of habits in life, then the results would be outstanding.

When something is not right for you, universe will keep you away from that thing.

So what meant for you will be yours.

If it is not meant for you, then universe will hold you back to get that thing.

So just smile that if you didn't get something then that would be right for you.

Universe knows that what is right and what is wrong for you.

Trust the Universe.

One day you will thank the universe that it didn't happen.

Universe always gives you that thing that you are capable of and you can handle it.

If you want something from universe then you have to be capable for that.

You have to show your qualities to the Universe.

Whatever you give to the Universe, Universe will give you back.

If you spread love, you will get Love.

If you spread kindness, you will get Kindness.

So make sure to give good to the Universe, same thing you will get back.

Whatever the circumstances are in your life, it can only be created by you.

Don't blame anyone for your situation.

Instead ask yourself that how I entered in this situation.

So your life depends on how your actions are towards your life and towards your Goals.

9 798889 322211